Heaven/Now

Heaven/Now

by
Leslie F. Brandt

with art by
Corita Kent

Publishing House
St. Louis

Other Now/Series books by Leslie Brandt
PSALMS/NOW
EPISTLES/NOW
JESUS/NOW
PROPHETS/NOW
MEDITATIONS/NOW

The Scripture quotations in this publication are from The Holy Bible: NEW INTERNATIONAL VERSION, © 1973, 1978, 1984 by the International Bible Society. Used by permission of Zondervan Bible Publishers.

Selected quotations are from the following books also authored by Leslie Brandt: *Psalms/Now,* copyright © 1973 Concordia Publishing House; and *Prophets/Now,* copyright © 1979 Concordia Publishing House.

Library of Congress Cataloging-in-Publication Data

Brandt, Leslie F.
    Heaven/now / by Leslie F. Brandt; with art by Corita Kent.
    ISBN 0-570-04582-7
    1. Future life—Meditations. 2. Death—Religious aspects—Christianity—Meditations. I. Corita, 1918–   II. Title.
    BT902.B74   1992
    236'.2—dc20   92-11938

1 2 3 4 5 6 7 8 9 10 PB 01 00 99 98 97 96 95 94 93 92

Dedicated to the Class of '41
of Augsburg College
who, along with me,
are soon to experience
that life beyond death
when God's glorious kingdom
will be fully realized

Contents

Preface

Norman Cousins once wrote: "The writer is similar to the theologian in at least one respect. He seeks to meet the hunger in people for immortality. That is, the writer's art is measured by his ability to transcend personal memory. Memory is the proof of life. Nothing really happens to a man unless it becomes memory. Some people pass through life in a state of total antisepsis: they have not touched life nor have they been touched by it. The artist-writer refines the ability of an individual to have contact with life, to be at one with others, to make their memories his own. In this sense, the writer widens the path to the subconscious and makes it possible for memories to take hold that would otherwise be barred. A writer, therefore, is something of a therapist. For his is the art that provides a person with fruitful solitude—sometimes in the heart of a crowd. The writer gives a man a chance to knit himself together. The psychologists call it integration, but all it means is that at some time a man must be capable of facing himself." (from *National Forum*).

Whatever the measure of my abilities as a writer, it is the purpose of this little volume to challenge and encourage people to face up to themselves, and especially, with their mortality as human beings. Nothing is more certain in life than our ultimate demise. Whereas Christians ought not and need not have any fear of their faith-journey's final chapter, they do have apprehensions, and need the encouragement of their brothers and sisters in the Christian faith. I hope this volume might be successful in confronting the final event and eliminating the fear, as well as celebrating the certainty of this journey's finality.

Leslie F. Brandt

Our Final Appointment

The fool says in his heart,
*   "There is no God."*—Ps. 14:1

Man is destined to die once,
*   and after that*
*   to face judgment.*—Heb. 9:27

"How foolish are the creatures of God!
They accumulate wealth and imagine
        themselves secure with
        their possessions and property.
Or they utilize some inborn gift
        and dote on the plaudits
        of their peers.
They live for themselves
        alone and give no thought
        to eternity.
They claim that God is simply not
        necessary to their existence.
They don't need the extra
        baggage of faith or religion.

But when the riches melt away,
        health fails,
        talents wear thin, and
        remaining years become few,
        when no one honors them or
        expresses concern for them,
        they stand naked and exposed

in empty despair.
Their fortress is breached;
    they are flattened and defeated.
Life, what little of it there is left,
    no longer has meaning for them.
They may look
    desperately for the God whom they
    may have discarded in their youth."
                    (Adapted from *Psalms/Now*)

Life truly is unfair;
    for many it is shockingly
    unjust and unequal.
Even for those of us who fortunately
    escape the terrible
    tragedies that befall
    millions throughout our world,
    we are bombarded
    daily with news and views of the
    atrocities and catastrophes
    perpetrated
    upon this world's population.
The carnage and pain
    of perpetual wars,
    the suffering and dying
    of the young and the very young,
    the diseases that ravage the multitudes,
    the oppressions and iniquities
    inflicted upon the masses,
    the constant threat of nuclear annihilation,
    and the list of horrors
    goes on and on.

Is there any wonder that,
 possibly more now than ever before,
 there are increasing
 numbers of people on our planet who
 are consciously facing
 up with their mortality and,
 in view of their personal inequities
 and their obvious lack of fulfillment
 during their lives upon earth,
 are wondering if death really is
 the end of human existence?

"It is hard to have patience
 with people who say
 'There is no death,' or
 'death doesn't matter,' "
 wrote C. S. Lewis
 following the death of his wife.
 "There is death. . . . And
 whatever happens has consequences,
 and it and they are
 irrevocable and irreversible. . . .
 Cancer, and cancer,
 and cancer. My mother,
 my father,
 my wife. I wonder
 who is next in the queue?"
 (From *A Grief Observed*)

Jesus wept when He was
 told about the death of His
 dear friend Lazarus.
Before His own death on the cross,

13

He cried out,
"My God, my God, why
have you forsaken Me?"
And before His last
breath He prayed,
"Father, into Your hands
I commit my spirit."

How bleak is the logic
of the secular humanists!
They may passionately hold to the intrinsic
worth of every human being.
They enthusiastically clamor
for personal fulfillment as
the highest goal
in the relatively short time
they spend on this planet.
Yet, even in the face of the gross
inequalities and
injustices and
sufferings that run
rampant amongst earth-dwellers,
there is for them no recourse beyond
the grave.
There really is no choice
when they face the ultimate end
of this existence
save some kind of self-made stoicism,
suicide, or cynicism and despair.

While "faith is being sure
of what we hope for and certain
of what we do not see" (Heb. 11:1),

the followers of Christ
ought to discover,
by the grace of God, the power
to confront their mortality and lay hold
of the assurance that
they are immortal.
While they may be somewhat apprehensive
in respect to this life's final moments,
they realize that they can face death
without fear.

There is, however, even for Christians,
some logic in the concept of immortality.
If there is any purpose for
and meaning in life as
experienced in our world,
it is illogical to assume that
death is the end
of human existence.
How can anyone even accept personhood
in this life and still deny
personal immortality?
It simply doesn't stand to reason
to believe that our
demise shuts out our
relationship to our Creator
for all eternity.
Thank God, it does not!

"What man can live
and not see death?"
queried the psalmist.
We cannot entirely reduce death's grotesque

ugliness or
minimize its horror.
Most of us will not forget
our first childhood contact
with it, nor the shock and pain
of its brutal invasion
of our family circles.
Despite the poet's attempts to picture
death as a sweet slumber,
or Forest Lawn's endeavors
to glamorize it;
despite the philosophers with their explanations,
the preachers and their promises,
there is a horror
about death that strikes fear into
the hearts of many people,
and most of us may not
completely rid ourselves of its
insidious threat to our beings.
As surely as comes the end of summer,
so surely must we face up to
the fact of death,
the parting of the way,
its incomprehensible darkness.

It is the Christian faith
that responds to this
ultimate anxiety.
Our Christ not only faced it,
bluntly and biologically,
He was victorious over it.
He transformed it from an enemy
bent on our destruction

into a friend that promises
to usher us into
eternal glory.
While this was certainly true
in respect to the death of Christ,
it also holds true
in respect to the deaths of
Paul and Peter and
James and the other apostles.
There are an unnumbered multitude who followed
in their footsteps.
Their deaths were not always sudden
or violent,
but they were significant.
As the blood of the martyrs
made fertile the soil for the
growth of the church, so
the lives and deaths of God's
faithful children serve
to extend God's Kingdom and
to accomplish His purposes.

This, then, is our concern:
not that we shall die,
for that we shall,
but that we may face that
coming event without fear
and even dare to believe and to pray
that our living
and our passing
will bring benefit and blessing
to others who follow behind.

"Let us consider carefully
    the security of a loving
    relationship to God.
Let us mouth His praises and
    demonstrate in our lives
    the eternal joy of knowing
    and relating to Him.
We need not depend on this world's
    wealth nor the accolades
    of human beings about us.
We need not fear the end
    of our days upon this earth.
God is forever—
    and so the souls of those who
    are committed to Him.
Clap your hands; shout for joy!
God is real, and He is here!"
    (Adapted from *Psalms/Now*)

Death—From Life to Life

[Jesus] touched the coffin . . . He said,
"Young man, I say to you,
get up!"
The dead man sat up
and began to talk.—Luke 7:14–15

This is one instance of
        the way our Lord dealt with
        human grief and death.
It should assure God's children
        of His power in respect
        to their lives, and
        to eradicate once and for always
        their fear of
        this ultimate event.

Death is
        one single step from the
        front stoop of this three-dimensional world
        before God lifts us up
        into the heaven of everlasting
        union with God—a step
        that Christians may well anticipate but
        certainly need not fear.

The fact is, we are not likely to be
        of much use to God
        in this world unless our eventual exodus

through death,
though at times fraught with apprehension,
holds no real fear for us.
"Do not weep," Jesus compassionately exhorted
the mother of the deceased man.
"Stop crying," He is saying
to doubting, sorrowing,
fearful, complaining
Christians today.
"Get up!" He said
to the deceased man and
is saying to all who claim His salvation
and yet are sick unto death
amidst the pains and pressures
of our uncertain and
insecure world.

Is it possible that some
of us still haven't learned how
to live, how
to lay hold of the love and life made
available through Jesus Christ
and His death on the cross,
a life that grants His supernatural peace
and joy
even in the midst of doubt
and pain and insecurity?
It is only when we "get up" and live
in the joy and power
of the resurrected Christ
that we can lovingly and helpfully respond to
the doubts and fears,
the burdens and sufferings,

of dying people about us.
It is when we do this that we are
    really living.

"Never send to know for whom the bell
    tolls; it tolls
    for thee," wrote John Donne.
"Man is destined
    to die once, and after
    that to face judgment,"
    declared the Scriptures (Heb. 9:27).
Everyone meets death—
    sooner or later,
    in one way
    or another.
Some meet it
    grandly, a speech in hand.
Some talk about it
    as if going to a long-delayed banquet.
Some sputter in the face of death
    like a wet fuse.
Some are impatient and belligerent;
    others are bewildered.
Some are stoic
    and attempt to be philosophical about it.
Some die with human dignity and grace,
    others with fear, even terror.
I have been with many people on the threshold of this
    unknown journey that they must take alone.
I have found, again and again, that those who face it
    with courage bathed in hope
    are those who have come to
    terms with it and have found

in the crucifixion
and resurrection of Christ
meaning and purpose in the prospect of death.
Yet it was Jesus Himself who paradoxically proclaimed:
"I tell you the truth,
if anyone keeps My word,
he will never see death" (John 8:51).
In these concise words He
addressed Himself to the greatest and most profound
contradiction of life:
that, whereas, everyone shall die,
there is no real death
for those who are in Christ Jesus.
"For Christ's love compels
us, because we are convinced that
one died
for all, and therefore all died,"
wrote Paul (2 Cor. 5:14).
And to Timothy, he wrote:
"If we died with Him,
we will also live
with Him" (2 Tim. 2:11).

"Limited awareness of one's own eventual death can be
the teacher of wisdom about how to live," wrote
a professor of religion.
"Teach us to number our days aright,
that we may gain
a heart of wisdom,"
sang the psalmist (Ps. 90:12).
Yet, strange as this may seem,
it has been reported that a majority
of funerals, most of which were

conducted by clergy,
strongly expressed our culture's denial
of death.
It is no wonder, then, that in this
atmosphere of denial
most people have serious difficulty
not only in relating
to the dying but also in
imagining their own mortality,
and this in spite of the fact that
religious traditions have assigned
much importance to being aware
of one's own death.
The ancient counsel to "know thyself"
meant above all
to know one's
self as mortal—
that each and every one of us must
someday conclude
this life's journey by dying.
Death is decisive; it is final.
It is decisive
in its absolute certainty;
it comes to all
and, in this respect, makes us all
equal.
Having understood this, however,
we can, with Kierkegaard, accept the fact
and recognize death as
the "master
teacher who can teach us
how to live."
Even though Jesus,

when hearing about Lazarus' death,
proclaimed that "whoever lives
and believes in Me will
never die," He would not deny
Lazarus' death;
but, for the sake of Lazarus' sisters,
raised him from the dead,
knowing full well that
Lazarus would eventually
face death for the second time.
For each of us, however, there is only
one death,
and as far as earth-life is concerned,
it is final.

Death for a Christian need not be
an ugly, atrocious thing,
although the manner in which some people
are forced to die
is most certainly so.
A child of God,
while sometimes apprehensive about it,
need not contemplate death with horror.
In carrying on the grand adventure of life
now and in eternity,
we, after Eden, know that
death is our reality
and is, in reality,
a step between
birth and rebirth in the resurrection.
We have divinely instilled within us the urge for
totality,
completeness,

perfect fulfillment.
This calls for a growth and development that comes
     only at the price of death.
"My life is a mystery,"
     someone has said,
     "but death is a
     dark malady
     which faith cannot evade.
     Yet faith has a
     word. It speaks
     of process and purpose of which death
     is a part, and it speaks
     of something steady over all
     the wreckage."

Every person must die for himself or herself,
     and that person must die
     alone.
But this is only the first death,
     the discarding of this mortality,
     the putting off of these human garments
     with all of the
     pains and sufferings,
     weaknesses and frustrations.
The second death,
     that eternal death that perpetually
     destroys, no man or woman need experience.
This death has been substituted for—
     by the death of Jesus Christ.
Because He died and rose from the dead,
     no one needs to die
     the second death.
The children of God can face death

without fear because they have
the hope of new life after death.
They shall live again:
joyfully,
purposefully,
eternally,
unrestrained
by the conflicts and contradictions
that are an integral part of life
in this world.

An author and educator,
who does not believe in personal immortality,
still believes that death is a friend of humankind.
"The human race could never have evolved without the great
institution of death," this author states.
"Death is the balancing element which remains today the
most important factor in keeping the world from being
smothered by overpopulation. . . . Death is a genuine
friend of humankind. . . . It always involves tragedy—
to the individual who dies, to family and friends,
to the community that person has served. . . . But
the sting of death can be tempered by realizing the full
creative role of death in nature" (author unknown).
And Walt Whitman once wrote: "I will show that nothing can
happen more beautiful than death."

Whether expressed by honored poets or contemporary authors,
it is doubtful that such offers much comfort for any of
us who are confronting our own mortality today.
Christians, however, do have a consoling conviction about
their immortality and, with Paul the apostle, can give
thanks to God who "gives us the victory through our

Lord Jesus Christ" (1 Cor. 15:57).
This is not a victory over death, but
a victory beyond death,
which we can even now celebrate because,
while the bodies we now inhabit will disintegrate,
we shall live eternally with spiritual bodies,
for "death has been swallowed up in victory."

A young lady who had been fighting
a continuous battle with
leukemia for three years said:
"Sometimes it seemed that
the disease had control and that
it would only be a matter of time before
death could laugh in triumph at me."
Being a Christian, she knew
of course
that death cannot
laugh at the decease of a child of God.
As much as it appears to be
so tragic to many in our world,
especially accidental or extremely painful deaths,
and certainly to loved ones who are
the real losers in such an event,
the death-dealing demon does not laugh;
for death for a Christian is
followed by an eternal
celebration in the Kingdom of our loving and
life-giving God.

I read about Ruthie and Verena one day.
They were born as conjoined twins.
While they had two completely different personalities,

they shared the same single heart.
They were joined together from the sternum to the navel.
It was impossible to separate them,
    and doctors said it would be a miracle if they
    lived out the year.
They lived for seven years.
According to their mother, they were happy children.
While they had distinctly different personalities,
    they complemented each other in amazing ways.
They even discovered how to alternate days
    on which each would make
    the decisions for that day.
They went to an elementary school,
    sang in a church choir,
    and biked together on a special tricycle.
After their seventh birthday, Ruthie's lungs,
    having deteriorated over several weeks,
    finally gave out; and she died.
Verena knew that she also would die,
    and she talked about it,
    stating that
    "This is the time we're going to be dying."
She instructed her mother to give her a list of friends
    that she wanted to give flowers to,
    and she asked that
    she be cremated "because
    she didn't want to be in a box;
    she wanted to be free."
And then, fifteen minutes after Ruthie had died,
    Verena breathed her last breath and followed her
    sister into eternity.

Our dying may not be as simple and peaceful as the passing

of Ruthie and Verena,
but it could be—
if we could truly embrace the words of
Jesus, who said, "I am the resurrection and the life.
He who believes in Me will live, even though he dies;
and whoever lives and believes in Me will never die"
(John 11:25–26).
"I have no fear of death," said Dale Bjork,
a beloved friend of mine during our missionary days in
northern China. "There's about the same amount of dread
as I would have if I were going to the dentist.
My faith is in the promise of God. I believe in the
hereafter. There's no uncertainty."
A few months later, Dale died
of amyotrophic lateral sclerosis.
Henri Nouwen, in a *Letter of Consolation* to his father
following the death of his mother, wrote:
"Mother's death encourages us to give up the illusions
of immortality we might have and to experience in a new
way our total dependence on God's love. . . .
We are called to meditate, not just on death in general
or on our own death in particular,
but on the death of Jesus Christ
who is God and man. We are challenged to look at Him
dying on a cross and to find there the meaning of our
own life and death. . . . Jesus of Nazareth did not die for
Himself, but for us, and that in following Him we too
are called to make our death a death for others. What
makes you and me Christian is not only our belief that
He who was without sin died for our sake on the cross and
thus opened for us the way to His heavenly Father,
but also that through His death our death is transformed
from a totally absurd end of all that gives life its

meaning into an event that liberates us and those
whom we love. . . ."

As Christians, we have, through the death
and resurrection of Jesus Christ, been granted
the gift of immortality,
but such comes into full bloom only after
we reach the end of our mortality and
through our death are separated
and liberated from our earth-
bound bodies to move into our spiritual bodies
and into the eternal presence of our Creator
and Redeemer (1 Cor. 15:42–43).

Shortly before he died, Dr. Paul Rees wrote:
"I shall go to my grave unshakable in the faith-
confession that, all appearances to the contrary,
'Jesus is Lord.' "
It is this same "faith-confession" that can envelop and
sustain our lives as we continue on our journey.

He Is Not Here; He Has Risen

Where, O death,
is your victory?
Where, O death,
is your sting?—1 Cor. 15:55

If only for this life we have hope in Christ,
we are to be pitied more than all men.—1 Cor. 15:19

Christians who relish
     mountaintop experiences and often
     have such hours or days in their lives
     may testify that even
     if heaven or immortality were not
     a clear-cut guarantee, they would find
     their relationship to the resurrected Christ
     rich and meaningful.
It would not be enough for the apostle Paul.

There is for Christians an indefinable but
     indestructible link between them
     and their union with the Creator
     beyond the bounds of this earthbound
     existence.
If Christ had not been raised from the dead,
     neither His words nor His deeds would be
     known to us today.
The title of Christian would not even exist.
It was because of Christ's resurrection that
     His two-thousand-year-old words and acts

are broadcast to every
country, city, and hamlet on this planet—
and will continue to be
as long as this globe continues
to circle the sun.
Our great God, Creator and Redeemer,
did not make us to be
playthings for His own amusement,
but to be His children united
to Him for all eternity.
We were made by God and for God.
Fulfillment can be discovered or achieved
partially in this life and totally in the next,
only if we return to God
and allow Him to have His way
with us.
We are recruited, redeemed, and reconciled
to God through
Jesus Christ
to be His children and ministers in the
kingdom of this world.
We are guaranteed everlasting life
within His love and purposes
in that Kingdom that He is preparing for us.
We become an integral part of that Kingdom when
we leave this planet through
death by giving up our mortality here
to become immortally the subjects and servants of
God.
The high point,
the constantly recurring theme,
and the grand climax in the great symphony
of the Gospel,

is the resurrection of our Lord, Jesus Christ.
He died for our sins, and He arose from the dead
    victorious
    over sin and death.
If we subtract this from our message
    of love and hope, we really have
    nothing to say.
There would be no hope of life after death,
    of immortality,
    or of heaven.
We would clutch desperately to the small
    joys and thrills
    of this all-too-short term on our planet
    and would terminate our existence
    amidst the pains and problems,
    the aches and agonies
    from which we cannot find relief.
We must be sure of this:
    the resurrection of Jesus Christ—
    and we can be.
    It was witnessed
    by many before us.
What is even more important,
    it has or can be experienced within us.
The resurrection of Jesus Christ assures us
    of our own personal resurrection.
It begins even now
    with the gift of immortality when
    we are born again
    through faith in Christ.
It is culminated in that eternal
    life and experience that follows
    our exodus from this world.

Among the great freedoms that we celebrate
        as Christians
        is our freedom from the fear of death.
Death is not the end but
        really the beginning.
It is not termination but promotion.
And this we know—because Jesus arose from the dead.
We shall, indeed, be raised from the dead.
Our God has not given
        to us the explanation of just
        how it shall be done.
But this we know:
        the perishable shall become imperishable
        and the mortal will become immortal
        on that great Day.

It is not surprising that we are
        often uneasy, frustrated, even angry
        about the atrocious things that happen
        in the world about us.
Almost every newscast violates
        our sensibilities,
        even to the point that we want to cry out
        for divine intervention in this
        planet's sad state of affairs.
The world is,
        by all appearances, well
        on its way to self-annihilation;
        and the children of God appear
        to be helpless and incapable
        of arresting its mad rush to extinction.

"Be patient, then, brothers, until the Lord's coming,"

said the apostle James (5:7).
Neither James nor any other of the apostles held any
    high hopes for the world as such.
Their hopes and their faith were in the promises and
    purposes of God as revealed
    to them through Jesus Christ.
"Be patient . . . because the Lord's coming is near" (James 5:8).
Take courage, be strong, shore up your heart,
    the coming of the Lord is at hand!
It is probable that
    little will be accomplished in fretting
    about this world's condition or even praying
    for Christ's immediate return.
It is important that we recognize the Christ who
    came at Christmas, who
    died on Good Friday, who
    arose from the dead on Easter, who
    sent His Spirit at Pentecost, and who
    is even now indwelling our lives.
Knowing this, we need daily
    to dedicate our lives to
    carrying out our Lord's objectives,
    which will eventually resolve
    in His grand intervention
    at the end of time.

What about that great Day in which God's Kingdom
    shall be revealed (Rev. 21:10)?
Is there any way we can picture that glorious event?

Some have had visions; others dream dreams.
But it is not possible
    for our small minds to visualize

the glory of God's eternal Kingdom.
Our imaginations are
    utterly incapable of grasping the
    majesty, beauty, and power of the glory
    that awaits the children of God
    on that great Day.
We see but minute glimpses of His eternal
    glory in the elements
    about us, yet even these are beyond the
    comprehension of our finite thinking.
The pictures we compose are crooked
    lines, abstract
    blobs that barely represent
    ultimate truth.
This, however, we believe:
    With the dawn of that magnificent Day,
    Christ shall be revealed
    in all His glory and majesty.
All the hosts of heaven will be
    gathered to sing His praises.
And every human creature upon this earth,
    along with those who have gone before us,
    will know that this one,
    who walked among us,
    who revealed God's eternal
    love and suffered in His own
    body the consequences of our
    faithlessness and disobedience—
    this one, the resurrected Christ,
    is Lord and King
    of this earth,
    the universe,
    of heaven itself,

for all eternity.
Only those of us who love and serve our God
    today can be assured of rejoicing in
    His manifestation tomorrow.
We can regard that great coming event with joyful
    anticipation.
May the "praise and glory and wisdom and thanks
    and honor and power and strength be to our God
    for ever and ever. Amen!" (Rev. 7:12).

"Do not rejoice that the spirits submit
    to you, but rejoice that your names are
    written in heaven" (Luke 10:20).
There is indeed reason
    for rejoicing, because our significance
    before God is not dependent on the feelings
    or the facts concerning our successes.
Our joy as the children of God is
    not to be measured
    by our accomplishments or achievements.
We are significant
    apart from such successes
    because we are
    rightly related to God through faith in Christ,
    walking in obedience to Him.
How do we *know* that
    our names are written in heaven?
    By knowing that we are
    the forgiven and accepted
    sons and daughters of God.
"You forgave the iniquity of Your people
    and covered all their sins,"
    proclaimed the psalmist (Ps. 85:2).

"There is now no condemnation for those who are
        in Christ Jesus," wrote Paul (Rom. 8:1).
Of course, we must bring our iniquities and wrongdoings
        to God.
We must recognize and receive the glorious
        message and gift of salvation:
        that Jesus Christ has already suffered
        the consequences of sin and guilt
        on our behalf.
We are to entrust our lives
        wholly and totally
        to the eternal
        promises of God as proclaimed in His Word.
We are to accept these promises and the Christ
        of these promises—
        and then to rejoice in this
        relationship of faith in God.
"Dear friends, now we are children of God,"
        wrote John (1 John 3:2).
Truly, this is reason for rejoicing!

Someone once pointed out that Jesus, as a Jew,
        did not have the Greek view of history.
He viewed it not as a never–ending circle
        but as a straight line with
        a beginning and an end.
Someday, there will be no tomorrow—
        as far as this existence is concerned.
The door will open, and then it will
        shut.
It is not a popular view in our times;
        it is virtually impossible to live
        every day as if there will be

no tomorrow.
"Look at the . . . trees,"
said Jesus to His disciples.
"When they sprout leaves, you can see
for yourselves
and know that summer is near. Even so,
when you see these things happening,
you know that the kingdom of God
is near. . . .
This generation will certainly not pass away
until all these things have happened. . . .
Be careful, or your hearts will be weighed down
with dissipation . . ." (Luke 21:29–32, 34).
The church has waited
ever since Pentecost
for Christ's return.
But it is difficult to stand on tiptoe
for 2,000 years,
awaiting that greatest of events.
The result is that we are tempted to live
as if there will always be a tomorrow.
Only fools can live like that,
and such are plentiful.
Conscientious people do think about
the end of life as they know it
and live with it on our planet.
With the serious ecological crises,
the threat of nuclear war,
the famines, deadly diseases,
disastrous events that haunt and harass us,
how can we not think in apocalyptic terms?

The Second Coming of Jesus Christ is

a heavily underscored
doctrine throughout the New Testament.
It could happen
at anytime, and certainly does
mean the end
of things as we have known them
on this planet.
Nevertheless, it is more than likely
that the end of our lives
upon this earth will precede that
great and final event that
will be initiated by
the return of our Lord Jesus Christ.
This we know well:
life on this globe will come to an end—
and this may be sooner than we think.

We are living in the shadows.
The gaiety, the prosperity,
the sensuality and superficiality about
us do not succeed in obliterating
those shadows of hunger, unemployment,
disease, drug addiction,
family breakups, wars,
corruption in high places,
death-dealing catastrophes
throughout the world.
We have the ominous feeling that these shadows are
prophetic harbingers of things to come.
We no longer assume that
the world will go endlessly on
like an everflowing stream.
Prophesying is no longer confined

to Biblical writers and
preachers who paint lurid and frightening pictures
of what we may all be facing.
Scientists, statesmen, educators are raising their voices
in warnings of the eventual
doom that awaits us.
"I see more evidence of impending doom
on the front page of my newspaper than
I hear about from the pulpits of
our churches," exclaimed one editor.
"There will be signs
in the sun, moon and stars,"
Jesus said.
"On the earth,
nations will be in anguish
and perplexity at the roaring
and tossing of the sea. Men will faint
from terror, apprehensive
of what is coming on
the world . . . " (Luke 21:25–26).
God's creatures are living in the shadows.

"Be careful, or your hearts will be
weighed down with dissipation,
drunkenness, and the anxieties of life,
and that day will close on you
unexpectedly like a trap.
For it will come upon all
those who live on
the face of the whole earth"
(Luke 21:34–35).
It is time to wake
up and look up, for

salvation is nearer
today than it has ever been before.
"Yes, I am coming soon" (Rev. 22:20).
This was the message from Christ that John heard
and which he sent to his persecuted, imprisoned,
suffering brothers and sisters in the faith.
This continues to be
the message of hope and comfort
for those of us who are
clinging to our faith and our lives
in the violent world of our generation.
Hold on! Hang in there! Jesus is coming soon!
While contemporary prophets often twist John's Revelation
into saying or meaning something never intended
by the writer,
the promise of an ending to violence, nuclear warheads,
devastating diseases, mass starvation, and all that is
evil and ugly is made known with the declaration of
our Lord's Second Coming.
There will be healing and joy, peace and rest,
for those who "hold on" in faith,
who allow God to hold on to them,
and who walk in obedience with
the invisible Christ who stays
with us all the way,
and continues to assure us that He is "coming soon."

"The hour has come for you
to wake up from your slumber,
because our salvation is
nearer now than when we first believed"
(Rom. 13:11).
Now is the time to get up

and "clothe yourselves with
the Lord Jesus Christ (Rom. 13:14).
"The night is nearly over;
the day is almost here,"
wrote Paul (Rom. 13:12).
While he warned against date-setting,
and even reprimanded some
of his readers for giving up
their jobs and normal responsibilities
to thumb-twiddle on
some holy hill awaiting
Christ's promised return,
he was filled with anticipation concerning
that great and ultimate event.
In the meantime,
God's children are
to live and act as if
His Kingdom has already been revealed,
the sun already risen;
for, even while there is darkness
and devastation about us,
Christ has come,
the Kingdom of God is here.
We are to "put aside
the deeds of darkness" (Rom. 13:12)
and live and love,
minister and serve,
as God's sons and daughters
are destined to do.
It is this grand announcement that ought to help
us dispel our fears and
to fill our beings with joy as we continue
on our journey of faith.

When the Journey Is Almost Over

Do not cast me away when I am old;
do not forsake me when
my strength is gone.—Ps. 71:9

Said the little boy, "Sometimes I drop my spoon."
Said the old man, "I do that too."
Said the little boy, "Sometimes I wet my pants."
"I do that too," laughed the old man.
Said the little boy, "I often cry."
The old man nodded, "So do I."
"But worst of all," said the boy,
    "it seems that grownups don't
    pay attention to me."
And he felt the warmth of a wrinkled hand.
    "Know what you mean," said the old man.
                  (Author unknown)

I and many of my readers are facing the last
    few months or years of our earthly journey and,
    according to Erasmus,
    "With our cares of mind
    purged away we become by gentle
    stages young again . . . ,
    [and] while sitting on the wall
    watching the rat race of
    sleek young warriors,
    [we] utter gracious and elegant discourses."
Maybe our discourses are seldom elegant.

Nevertheless, if we are to believe Erasmus,
  "The farther we proceed in age
  the nearer we come back to the semblance
  of childhood, until, like children
  indeed, having no weariness
  of life or sense of death,
  we take leave of the world . . ."
It is then that the precious words of our Lord
  return to cheer us:
  "Let the little children come to Me . . .
  for the Kingdom of God belongs to
  such as these" (Luke 18:16).
For us there is indeed heaven
  now and in our future.
We need not fret nor need we fear,
  for we are the children of God.
"Even youths grow tired and weary,
  and young men stumble and fall;
  but those who hope in the Lord
  will renew their strength.
  They will soar on wings like eagles;
  they will run and not grow weary,
  they will walk and not be faint"
  (Is. 40:30–31).

Isaiah's advice is as relevant today
  as it has ever been:
  "Forget the former things;
  do not dwell on the past.
  See, I am doing a new thing!
  Now it springs up;
  do you not perceive it?
  I am making a way in the desert

and streams in the wasteland. . . .
Because I provide water in the desert
and streams in the wasteland,
to give drink to My people, My chosen,
the people I formed for Myself
that they may proclaim My praise" (Is. 43:18–21).

Even while we labor in the valley,
we desire to float above
the cloud-shrouded snowcapped
peaks that hover over its edges.
We are weary with running through desert sands,
and want desperately to soar.
St. Teresa of Avila once said:
"The further I journey in life—
God help me—
the less comfort I find."
Nor will we continually bask in comfort
on our journey of faith,
but we will always have
the grace of God to support
and sustain us—and grant us peace.
While anxiety is the result of
not knowing who we are
and to whom we belong,
we know who we are and to whom we belong.
"We are the children of God," declared John.
"Do not let your hearts be troubled.
Trust in God; trust also in Me,"
said Jesus (John 14:1).
"Even though [we] walk through the valley
of the shadow of death,
[we] will fear no evil,

for [God is with us],"
    proclaimed the psalmist (23:4).
"You will grieve, but your grief will
    turn to joy," said Jesus (John 16:20).
We may not be able to ignore
    the storm that rages
    or escape
    the conflicts that beset us
    or turn away from
    the heavy burdens that tax our strength.
We continue, however, to focus anew on that
    one who is in the midst of the storm,
    who will stand with us
    through our conflicts and who
    will not bend under
    the weight of our heavy burdens.

"The Lord is my light and my salvation—
    whom shall I fear?" sang the psalmist
    (Ps. 27:1).
While he was aware that life
    would never be a flower-strewn
    path, he encourages us
    to "be strong and take heart" (v. 14).
The road beneath us and before us is
    narrow and twisted,
    often steep and precipitous.
Evildoers assail us,
    hosts are encamped against us,
    and there may be times when even our loved ones
    may forsake us.
The way is often rough;
    the days are sometimes very dark.

We ought by now to be assured that God is
within us.
When we emerge from our little caves
of self-pity and despair,
we discover our brothers and sisters
in Christ traversing
this same road with us.
Our Lord may not lead us on
"level ground" as the psalmist once prayed (143:10),
but He continues to be
our light in the darkness that
swirls about us and
our salvation from whatever
may threaten us.
And the journey before us
leads to eternal splendor
and everlasting glory.

"Weeping may remain for a night,"
said the psalmist,
"but rejoicing comes in the morning"
(30:5).
That "morning" is about to dawn;
the Day of the Lord is soon upon us.

God grant us the grace to hold on,
to refresh ourselves
with the gracious, life-giving
waters He provides,
and to continue to proclaim His
praises as we continue our pilgrimage together.

What about *Heaven/Now?*

Do not rejoice that the spirits submit to you,
but rejoice that your names are
written in heaven.—Luke 10:20

When asked about what heaven will be like,
        Dennis the Menace responded:
        "Heaven probably looks like a toy shop, . . .
        sounds like a carousel, . . .
        and smells like a deli."
Dennis may be about as rational as any of us
        in any attempt to describe or explain
        that place or dimension that we
        assume exists somewhere above or beyond
        this planet on which we live.
It is true that many within the human family
        have little or no concern at all
        about immortality or
        the "great beyond."
They may refer to heaven
        as "pie in the sky by and by" even
        as they dedicate their life-endeavors
        to bringing justice and peace,
        joy and fulfillment to the creatures
        of this world.
Numerous cults gather around charismatic leaders who
        urge their followers to discover
        their own identities and
        celebrate the "god" within

them and who snub the "pie
in the sky" concept of heaven
to make for themselves a heaven
on earth.
While a great many of our fellow citizens are
thrill-and-instant-gratification seekers
thinking only about
their individual needs and desires,
others are possibly more devoted
to the welfare of the
oppressed and impoverished than those who
claim to follow Jesus Christ.
Then there are, unfortunately, even
some followers of Jesus who are
more concerned about preparing for another life
or their eternal existence than
they are about making life on this planet
bearable for themselves and others.
There are even those occasions when
the Christian's concepts of
immortality and life-in-the-hereafter are used
diabolically in zealous attempts
to offset or put down
the tragedies and pains so present and prevalent
in our world.
Most of the pain and suffering
that afflicts this world's creatures is
that which they inflict upon one another:
within or between families,
race against race,
nation against nation,
religion against religion.
The truly motivated disciples of Christ

discover and embrace their identity and value
as God's children and servants.
They also affirm
the worth and dignity of every human being
and proclaim an ultimate purpose for
each of God's creatures—
a purpose that guides, sustains, and propels
the children of God into
loving and serving relationships
with one another within the human family.
This purpose transcends
this life on earth and is ultimately
taken up and fulfilled in that everlasting
life that follows the Christian journey
upon this planet.
For mature Christians, this ultimate
hope of life everlasting, this
immortality, which is
God's gift to all of His children,
and which is proclaimed, granted,
and received through Baptism,
is indeed a consoling
factor under the ever-present shadow
of death.
Death, annihilation,
nonbeing, nonconsciousness,
the extinction of all the oppressions
and injustices
that befall people about us,
are regarded by some of our fellow beings
as the only way
to eternal peace.
How desolate it must be

for those who face the abrupt
termination of this life and of all
possibilities of fulfillment here
because they are not aware of the
precious gift of eternal life!
They have no conviction or concern
about that Kingdom that
even now has taken root
in the hearts of God's believing and beloved
children on this earth
and which will be totally
manifested in that place
or dimension referred to as
heaven.

Immortality and eternal life will remain
an inconceivable mystery
as long as we cling to the mortal coils
of our humanity.
We will continue to receive our consolation
by means of our God-given and Spirit-empowered
faith, which, according to the author of Hebrews,
"is being sure of what we hope for
and certain of what we do not see"
(11:1).
The object and basis of that faith is
the crucifixion and
resurrection of Jesus Christ.
There is sufficient evidence
in those historic events to
confirm and perpetuate those events
in my life and in the lives of millions
of Christ-followers

throughout our world.
While very few of our history books
cover or refer to it,
the lives of countless millions,
beginning with the men
and women who witnessed those events
and others who lived, suffered, and died
proclaiming the Christ of those events,
the grand and good news
of the death and resurrection
of Jesus Christ has been
proclaimed throughout the world
and embraced by men
and women everywhere.
The resurrection of Christ cannot be explained away;
it can only be ignored
by the hearts and minds
of unbelieving people.
Those who seriously grapple with
Christ's death and resurrection
and surrender to the risen Christ
can confront their mortality
without fear, for
"whoever lives and believes in
[Jesus] will never die" (John 11:26).
There may be other evidences of immortality—
the near-death experiences of some people, those
unnatural or transcendent episodes that are
occasionally experienced,
but it will always be
the resurrection of Jesus Christ
that forever cancels out
the victory and sting of death

(see 1 Cor. 15:54–57).

Immortality, eternal life, heaven
    are words that do not belong
    in a vocabulary that offers explanation or
    information or
    even reasoned inquiry and discourse.
They are symbolic rather than empirical,
    faith words;
    not literal language,
    and, if taken literally, are
    simply inconceivable.
To attempt to imagine ourselves endlessly
    enduring life, at least in view of our
    living as we do in this world,
    is simply beyond comprehension.
The words we use in respect
    to immortality and heaven point
    in the direction of the infinite
    and the transcendent
    while life and language here are bound
    to the limits of time.
They may suggest or proclaim
    but cannot define or explain that
    fulfillment Christians will discover and
    possess at the end of their
    journey on this planet.
Such words indicate faith's stammering
    attempts to grasp
    a concept of existence beyond death that will be
    real and fulfilling
    and not merely some kind of
    survival out of or salvation from
    the pain and suffering that has been

humanity's inheritance in this world.
While we need to face our mortality
and may reflect on what happens when
our part on life's stage is over,
we do not need to be preoccupied
with the hope of immortality, for immortality
has already been granted to
God's redeemed sons and daughters.
Such a reflection ought to result
in our commitment to God's purposes for
our lives here and now,
and in the elimination of our fears
in respect to our eventual
demise.

The World in Which We Live

In this world you will have trouble.
But take heart!
I have overcome the world.—John 16:33

Peace I leave with you;
My peace I give to you. . . .
Do not let your hearts be troubled
and do not be afraid—John 14:27

The world appears to be erupting about us.

Alien cultures are displacing the one
    in which we have our roots.
Revolutions, cataclysmic changes, upheavals
    of one sort or another
    have always been with us.
And until our great God winds up
    history as we know it, they
    shall always be with us.

We cannot any more avoid or ignore these
    disturbing events
    than did our Lord and His faithful
    followers in the face of
    Judah's harlotry or Rome's paganism.

Jesus knew full well what His followers would face.
He indeed promised peace that passes understanding.
He promises, as well, that those who labored

for His Kingdom would
face division, conflict, and persecution.
He led the way to the scaffold.
Most of His disciples followed closely behind.
He has gone that way before us,
    but only to return and,
    through His Spirit,
    to love and empower and bless
    us in the midst of these
    earth-shaking, soul-wringing events and
    to stay close beside us all the way on
    our journey of faith.

We may remember that incident
    when Jesus and His disciples
    were crossing the sea in a small boat.
A storm broke and the waves
    began washing into their vessel.
Jesus was sleeping, and
    the disciples became panicky and
    called out to Him to do something
    lest they all drown.
Awakening from His slumber,
    their Lord commanded the storm
    to abate—and there was
    dead
    calm.
Then He said to His disciples,
    "Where is your faith?" (Luke 8:25).

Our world, country, communities,
    even our churches
    are tossing about on tempestuous seas.

In the midst of all this we are
    often like those disciples—
    panic-stricken, frightened
    out of our wits,
    beating the air
    for something to which to cling.
Perhaps Christ is saying to us something
    of what He wanted
    to relay to those disciples:
    "Why are you such cowards?
    What little faith you have!
    I have created, redeemed, and appointed
    you for just such
    times as these. I will always be
    with you, indwelling
    you, empowering you, working out
    My will through you.
    Trust Me; I won't let you down.
    There is a quiet harbor somewhere
    at the end of your journey, but for now
    you are to abide in Me and to work for
    Me in the midst of stormy waters."

The Christian life is not
    a life without conflicts.
It has been that way from the beginning;
    it shall continue
    as long as God's creatures continue
    to inhabit our world.
Those people who float peacefully by, oblivious
    of or impervious to
    the conflict-ridden world about them,
    desperately clinging

to their precious ecstasies or
god-in-a-box concepts until Jesus comes
to take them to heaven,
are on the wrong ship.
Others may be stuck in some dull
and decadent harbor when
they should be sailing
the storm-tossed seas
of this planet's realities where
God's servants and fishers-of-men-and-women are
supposed to be.

We who are the redeemed children of God
    are the children of eternity.
We need not be afraid
    of what is transpiring about us or
    shocked into a debilitating numbness
    by the sweeping events of this
    day in which we live.
We must sometimes roll
    with the punches—to adjust, to adapt,
    and to respond
    in God-fearing, neighbor-loving ways to
    whatever happens on our course through life.
However, we do not have to be afraid.
    We are the objects
    of God's eternal, ever-present love;
    and we are His servants
    assigned to minister to our kind
    of world and to His creatures
    that live upon it.

Heaven/Now in This World in Which We Live

Be sure of this:
The kingdom of God is near.—Luke 10:11

Our Father in heaven . . .
Your kingdom come . . .
on earth as it is in heaven.—Matt. 6:9

The kingdom of the world
     refers to the activities and antics of sinful
     human beings on our planet,
     the arena within which the satanic,
     spiritual forces of evil are
     free to tempt, delude,
     seduce, and destroy the
     human creatures of God.

In the early Christian centuries,
     the term "Kingdom of God" was used
     to designate heaven itself—
     and this was often the meaning of
     the phrase even in the mouth of Jesus,
     and Jesus Himself was
     embodying that Kingdom,
     or heaven, in His own person.
I am convinced that,
     while interpretations of the Kingdom
     of God have been varied,
     it is synonymous with,
     or as close as we come to,

the meaning and existence of heaven.
Jesus, in the Lord's Prayer,
    identified heaven as the place of God
    and urged His disciples to pray that
    God's heaven or Kingdom
    and the will of the Father
    be made known upon earth.
    And He promised that the efforts of those who
    followed Him in seeking to make that happen
    would be rewarded
    in that world, that heaven to come.
This is the reason I dare to think
    and write about
    heaven *now*.

Inasmuch as the Kingdom of God is
    revealed to our eyes
    through the miracles of nature
    and to our ears amongst
    our interpersonal relationships,
    as well as through the transcendent
    or infinite whispers
    of another realm or universe
    by way of the genius of
    talented human beings,
    so in some measure is the realm of heaven
    revealed to us now.
We will never know or experience
    the fullness or totality of
    God's Kingdom or heaven
    while we abide upon this planet.
We might have fleeting glimpses of
    God's "hindquarters," but could never look

upon His face and live.
There will, however, be no doubt of
　　heaven's existence or
　　eternalness
　　once we leave this world behind
　　to be united with God
　　and His everlasting purposes.

How, then, can we recognize, experience,
　　and even identify heaven *now?*
　　It isn't likely that agnostics and unbelievers
　　in respect to the Christian faith
　　can ever do so.
Heaven may not be revealed to those
　　who refuse to accept and follow
　　Jesus Christ as their Savior and their King,
　　or they may be so blinded
　　by the bright lights of this
　　world's events and luminaries
　　that the light of heaven
　　becomes invisible to them.
"Wide is the gate
　　and broad is the road that leads to
　　destruction, and many enter through it,"
　　said Jesus,
　　"but small is the gate and narrow
　　the road that leads to life,
　　and only a few find it"
　　(Matt. 7:13–14).
It is when God's creatures bypass
　　the wide gates and broad roads of
　　their own self-centered aspirations and
　　ambitions and focus

their lives upon the sometimes
stern and often rough paths
of God's life and purposes that the
joy and love of heaven become very real
in both its earthly presence and
its future fulfillment.

The disciples of Jesus had some
remarkable experiences in
the short period of His earthly ministry.
While heaven and immortality were not
always or clearly understood
in early earthly Jewish history,
the Israelites were confronted
by the powers of heaven
in the crossing of the Red Sea,
the giving of the Law,
water obtained from a rock,
and manna from the skies.
Their immediate goals were
to reach the Promised Land as
the place where they could live
in freedom and grow into
a rich and powerful nation.
It was the healing miracles of Jesus,
the feeding of the five thousand,
the transfiguration on the mountain,
the resurrection of Christ,
the gift of the Holy Spirit,
that provided the disciples many
light-at-the-end-of-the-tunnel
glimpses of heaven that served to strengthen
them for living and serving

as well as to lessen their concerns about
dying.
Isaiah, that great prophet from
the Old Testament,
testified to having
had a genuine contact with heaven.
He saw the Lord
seated on the throne
amongst winged seraphs
flying about and singing the praises of
the Lord
Almighty.
This was enough to
drive the prophet to his knees
in confession
of his sins and the sins of his people
(Isaiah 6).
Paul, the apostle from the New Testament,
was on his way to capture and imprison
the followers of Jesus, when
"a light from heaven flashed around
him. He fell
to the ground and
heard a voice say
to him, 'Saul, Saul,
why do you
persecute Me?' "
(Acts 9:3–4).
Paul didn't *see* anything;
heaven's light had blinded him.
However, he heard
the voice from heaven;
and the experience completely changed

his life, and probably the
course of history.
Supernatural happenings continue
to bring joy and conviction
to some of God's children even today.

While heaven in all its glory has been
promised and will be disclosed
in God's own time, there are
faith-strengthening flashes
and whispers of its eternal glory
in the valleys as well as on
the mountains of the Christian journey
on this earth.
"Faith is being sure of what we hope for
and certain of what we do not see,"
wrote the author of Hebrews.
The followers of Christ are already
on the front stoop of
the heaven that beckons.
Death becomes that event or incident
that takes God's children
over the threshold into
the great banquet room of
God's heavenly and eternal glory and majesty.

As children of God, we see something better—
in the Word of God that is
proclaimed,
the sacraments that are
administered,
the glory of sunrises and sunsets,
the beauty of the flowers

that grow about us,
the power and peace of stormy and serene
oceans, in the grandeur of music
through instrument and song,
the "thousand points of
light" scattered over our night-skies.
There are but minute suggestions of heaven
in a Pacific sunset,
a Bach Chorale, or
in "surprises of joy" such as the
garden experience of C. S. Lewis.
But the Christian's faith is indeed
strengthened through these
reflections of the Ultimate and the Eternal.
What is even more amazing is the way
heaven is so often sensed through
Christian fellowship and love as we
live, work, worship, and play together.
Inasmuch as we are conduits and
channels of love to one
another, so we transmit something of
heaven's healing
and love and joy
to one another.

Credentialed for *Heaven/Now*

You did not choose Me,
but I chose you
and appointed you
to go and bear fruit—
fruit that will last.—John 15:16

How can we discover heaven *now,* and
        bring heaven's gifts and light
        into the darkness of our world—
        a world that appears at times
        to be "going to hell?"
How can we, mere mortals
        in this earthly kingdom,
        bear witness to the Kingdom of God
        in such times
        as these?

Jesus came to establish God's Kingdom—
        to bring to this world
        the blessings and benefits of
        heaven *now.*
He has credentialed
        and commissioned His disciples to
        carry on that task
        after He concluded His earthly ministry.

We who are the objects of
        His redeeming love and grace and

have dedicated our lives
to following Jesus Christ
have been blessed
with the responsibility of making heaven
now a reality
to humanity about us, and
we have become empowered to do this.
"Do you not know that
your bodies are members
of Christ Himself?"
wrote Paul.
"Do you not know that
your body is a temple of the
Holy Spirit, who is
in you, whom you have
received from God?"
(1 Cor. 6:15, 19).
"How great is the love
the Father has lavished on us,
that we should be called
children of God!
And that is what we are!"
(1 John 3:1).
At another time Paul wrote:
"Those who are led
by the Spirit of God are
sons [and daughters] of God" (Rom. 8:14).
We become God's heirs,
His very children,
through our Baptism.

This means we are
the very brothers and sisters of

Jesus Christ—and God's special people
to whom He has entrusted the task of
carrying on
the incarnation of Jesus Christ, which is
to bring God's Kingdom into the
kingdom of this world.
We are empowered
to do what Jesus would do
through us in terms of
relating His redemptive love to
the present-century inhabitants of this planet
and are the only means He has
of reflecting the beauty and power
and peace of heaven.

Before we can realize and
utilize our credentials as God's
children and effectively make known
heaven's gifts and blessings within
the kingdom of this world,
we must focus anew on that cross of
Christ, which became
the final consequence of His ministry in
this world's kingdom.
"How can I ever really celebrate Easter
without observing Lent?"
wrote Henri Nouwen
in his book of prayers.
"How can I rejoice fully in
Your resurrection when I have avoided
participating in Your death?
Yes, Lord, I have to die
with You, through You and in You . . .

and then become ready to recognize You
when You appear to me in your
resurrection."

(From A Cry for Mercy)

The roads that Jesus traveled
    in His earthly ministry always
    headed toward the cross.
This was the price He had to pay
    in order that God's Kingdom might be
    manifest in the kingdom of this world.
The prospect of dying for
    the sins of God's human creatures
    held little attraction for the human Christ.
The temptation had ever been present
    to turn aside and choose
    an easier path.
Satan himself once displayed before Christ
    the kingdoms of the world
    in all their glory
    with the promise:
    "All this I will
    give You, if
    You will bow down and
    worship
    me"
    (Matt. 4:9).
The devil, having the control
    that he has in this world's kingdom,
    was not able to detour Christ from
    the cross that He must endure
    at the end of His earthly journey.
While the cross of Christ was

not initially understood
by His disciples, and remains obscure
to our world at large,
and even to many who claim to
follow and serve the Christ today,
it was central
to Jesus' ministry and continues to be
for those who minister in His name
in this hour.
Neither heaven nor its eternal blessings
are available to those who seek
some easier or less offensive way of
securing heaven's favor.
Apart from the crucifixion of Christ,
there is no resurrection of Christ—
nor is there any
heaven for those who,
under the umbrella of
positive-thinking and New Age labels,
seek a religion that comforts and consoles
them in a world gone awry.

"May I never boast
except in the cross
of our Lord Jesus Christ,
through which the world has been crucified
to me, and I to the world,"
wrote Paul to the church at Galatia (Gal. 6:14).
"For I resolved to know
nothing while I was with you
except Jesus Christ and Him crucified,"
he said to the church at Corinth
(1 Cor. 2:2).

"But we preach Christ crucified . . . ,
     Christ the power of God and
     the wisdom of God" (1:23–24).
The cross of Christ,
     however, is not only central in our theology,
     it is to be constantly carried on
     in our ministry in
     the kingdom of this world.
After Jesus informed His disciples
     about what would happen
     to Him in Jerusalem, He said:
     "If anyone would come after Me,
     he must deny himself and
     take up his cross and follow Me"
     (Matt. 16:24).
A Lutheran theologian,
     Carl Braaten, writes:
     "The cross of Christ
     and the cross of the Christian
     cannot be separated.
     The glory of the Christian life in
     the world is hidden under the signs
     of suffering, humility, grief,
     disgrace, despair, and death.
     The place to go in
     following Jesus is not inside the
     walls of sacred institutions, but
     outside the gate where He experienced
     humiliation, forsakeness, and
     weakness. Such is the life
     of Christian discipleship;
     it leads into suffering—
     not the kind of suffering whereby

we work out our salvation by
acquiring merits exacted
by a righteous God, but the kind
of suffering that comes
from bearing the cross of Christ and
incurring the enmity of the world.
Such cross-bearing arouses
conflict and strife;
Christians ought to expect that
they will be regarded as sheep
for the slaughter.
Martyrdom is not a way
of salvation but the price
that Christians unavoidably pay in
doing hand-to-hand combat with
the forces of evil in the world.
The ethic of a Christian is
one of conformity to Christ,
and that means to take the
form of the servant in waiting on others."

(From *The Apostolic Imperative*)

What does this mean for us and
     our ministry, a ministry that will
     reveal God's Kingdom
     in the midst of this worldly kingdom
     and to bring heaven
     now in some measure
     into the desperate days and
     violent nights of our
     discordant world?
It means accepting our fellow beings
     where they are in order

that we may lovingly and
compassionately lead them to where
God wants them to be.
This means stooping
to the foot-washing level of our
neighbors' needs in order to
lift them to the heights of
God's loving and grace–giving acceptance.
It means to identify with humanity
about us irrespective of
class, color, or creed,
to be truly human yet
Spirit-led in the presence of
our brothers and sisters in the human family.
And this means our involvement with
the sufferings, the problems,
the conflicts and consternations,
the failures and defeats of
our fellow-persons—
to share one another's sorrows,
help bear one another's burdens.
It means that we put our lives
on the line
in loving and
sacrificial activities to bring
justice and dignity
and opportunity and validity
and the love and grace of God
to every human being within
our reach or circle of influence.

We are not to do these things
or reflect these attitudes

in order to *become* Christians,
we are to do such because
we *are* Christians and have been
immersed in God's forgiving love
and His righteousness,
through Jesus Christ and His cross.
All this is to be
the consequence of our salvation,
the taking up of our cross
on behalf of others even as
Jesus bore the burden of our sin
on His cross and
on our behalf.

The human creature is
born with an inferiority complex.
Many of God's creatures will spend
the better part of their lives
seeking to overcome it,
to discover worth and validity,
often through bizarre ways that only
drive them further from their Creator.
Through Christ we have been
restored to God's orbit,
reunited to God's family and Kingdom,
redeemed and adopted as His sons and daughters,
chosen to be the disciples of Jesus,
and committed to the eternal purposes
of the heavenly Father who
persistently seeks to bring
His heavenly Kingdom to
our sin-ridden planet.

Equipped for Service

His divine power has given us
everything we need for life
and godliness
through our knowledge of Him who
called us by His own glory and goodness.—2 Peter 1:3

Peter, in his second letter,
   was writing to a group of people who had
   suffered much in the world
   they encountered, and they wondered whether
   they had what it would take
   to face the kind of world that closed in
   around them.
In a world of computers
   and space shuttles
   and laser beams,
   of status quo, country-club religious institutions,
   of rebellious youth
   and oppressed minorities,
   of atheistic idealogies
   and fascist political philosophies,
   a world that could be destroyed
   instantly with a push-button war
   or gradually become extinct
   through the continued misuse
   and abuse of its natural resources,
   our first inclination may be
   to burrow into some dark hole

and pull it in after us.

Our natural faculties simply
do not enable us to face
this kind of world.
We admit to frustration,
if not outright fear,
and an agonizing feeling
of emptiness and inadequacy.
It is, therefore, not surprising that
many will join a cult
that awaits Christ's imminent return or
God's ultimate windup of history.
There are some who choose to
ignore the frightening things
taking place in the world about them and
focus upon the vague proposal that
they can be miraculously delivered
from the obscene consequences of
humankind's self-centeredness and
Satan's deviousness and,
without the troublesome event of death,
to be transported
to the eternal, joy-filled, peaceful
Kingdom in the sky—
while the world behind them goes
to hell.

Christ's return will take place—
today, tomorrow,
a decade or a century from now—
but we are
here and now.

We are appointed, commissioned, and
        credentialed for just such a time as this,
        and "His divine power has given us everything
        we need for life and godliness"
        here and now.
How do we go about
        accepting it, laying claim to it, and
        making it work in and through our lives?

How difficult to imagine that
        people can die of malnutrition with
        hundred-dollar bills stuffed
        into their mattresses! Yet
        it happens from time to time.
Spiritually stated, it can be
        a common malady among Christians.
While God stands by to provide all
        that is needed to live
        effective, contributive, joy-filled lives,
        His children are struggling
        with spiritual malnutrition.
Even if it is not verbalized,
        religious as well as
        not-so-religious people often
        question God's seeming limitations
        in our chaotic world today.
If God does limit Himself,
        it may be primarily because of
        the unbelief of His children or
        their unwillingness to take Him at His word.
He has no hands but our hands,
        and when they hang limp
        with unbelief or rigid

with fear, they are hardly
active in creating or healing or
channeling the promises and blessings of
God's heaven into the kingdom of this world.
Most of us do not have much
trouble with Christmas—
when heaven came into our midst
by way of the baby Jesus.
Pentecost, however, is still
one colossal mystery.
We are quite comfortable with the manger scene
and may even embrace
Easter and its grand tidings
of victory over sin and death,
but Pentecost is something totally
incomprehensible for many of us.
Heaven, though not in the total and
complete sense, is transmitted to us
through the Christmas, Good Friday,
and Easter experiences
in our lives, but even these are really
to prepare the way for
Pentecost, which is
the culmination of everything that happened
before it and is the key to God's
invisible and heavenly presence and
power in our world today.
Thus, Pentecost inaugurated the perpetual
presence of Christ in our world—
through us and our fellow-disciples
in the Christian faith.
Whereas Christmas means that
God became man,

Pentecost initiates
the event whereby men and women become
the vehicles and channels of God
and His heaven to our world.
The fact is, God's faithful children are
the only "Christs" that God has
to advance His Kingdom
and reveal His heaven
and carry out His purposes
on this planet.

We are in the midst of change and conflict
in a distorted world in order
to carry on the incarnation of God—
that He in His love for us
and through our love for others
may communicate and demonstrate divine
love and healing to
the lonely, unloved,
frightened, and fractured
people all about us.
The same power that brought the visible
Christ into our world
through the virgin Mary
and raised Him from the dead
on the Day of Resurrection is
that very same power,
that divine energy,
that abides within us.
This is our equipment, and it is
more than adequate for
the task that God has set before us.

The Joy of Heaven

With joy you will draw water
from the wells of salvation.—Is. 12:3

I have told you this so that
My joy may be in you
and that your joy may be complete.—John 15:11

Along with the equipment for
    the task at hand is the joy of being
    the children and servants of our great God.
It is truly the joy of heaven itself
    granted to us through
    His ever-present Spirit.
And yet that effervescence or ecstasy
    that accompanies the religious
    experiences of some people is
    neither the promise nor the proof of
    a Christian experience.
Even if it were possible
    to completely overcome our own conflicts,
    we are commissioned
    to share or to help bear
    the sufferings and sorrows of
    our fellow beings.

The fact is, however, that
    even while the boat rocks and the
    earth trembles and the heart is beset
    with doubts and fears, there is joy—

joy mixed with pain and depression
and the defeats and failures of our lives,
a joy that is sometimes
limited only by our unwillingness
or inability
to truly and persistently embrace God's
glorious gift of love and acceptance.
Our joy often may be tempered
by the agonies and sorrows of
our fellow creatures.
Nevertheless, it is the joy
of heaven, profound and eternal—
not self-induced or
the result of some inner chemistry,
nor dependent upon favorable circumstances—
but the gift of God that comes to everyone
who will receive it and respond to it.

There is reason for this joy.
Set free from sin's guilt and eternal consequences
and restored to God's orbit and
destiny for our lives, we are
His sons and daughters forever.
Even when we fail,
we belong to Him; and
He will never let us go.
There *is* a time for weeping and regretting—
but not for long.
The Christian experience is one of joy—
and only when our lives and our
worship services reflect this
will they offer any sort of attraction to the
unhappy, joyless world about us.

All this harks back to
    what we really believe about ourselves as
    God's sons and daughters.
When we really love and accept
    ourselves as God loves and accepts
    us, while this may or may not result in
    some out-of-this-world ecstasy,
    it will most certainly resolve into joy.

As Christians in a hostile world,
    we walk a sometimes difficult and
    discouraging path.
There are moments of ecstasy—
    a Beethoven symphony,
    a walk in the woods,
    an inspiring sermon,
    a conversation with a dear friend.
There are hours of pain and frustration—
    our own defeats,
    a friend or loved-one's suffering,
    our unmet or assumed needs,
    our apparently unfruitful endeavors.
But through it all
    there is joy—
    deep, profound, inexplicable joy.
This is the joy of knowing that we are
    God's children,
    God's servants and ministers,
    that all that is His is ours,
    and that we are His forever.

Bringing Heaven to Earth

Do not work for food
that spoils, but for food
that endures to eternal life.—John 6:27

A disciple of Christ,
> a servant or minister of God,
> is one, or one of many,
> who carries the power
> and purposes of God and who
> reflects and transmits
> the very peace and power of
> heaven into every phase
> or facet of society—
> to the rich and the poor,
> labor and management,
> the illiterate and educated—
> and who represents God
> and speaks and ministers
> for God in the industrial, commercial,
> governmental, educational, scientific,
> economical, political, medical
> complexes of society.
He represents heaven—
> and seeks to bring a bit of heaven
> into these complexes wherein he serves.
A true disciple is one who
> proclaims and demonstrates and
> makes applicable and relevant

God's love and heaven's gifts
for humanity through one-on-one
relationships that personalize that
love and those blessings
in very genuine responses to
the person next door, the coworker at the
office, the cantankerous
boss, the crabby neighbor,
a sick relative, a hungry child.
A disciple of Christ is one who
identifies with the person or persons
to whom he or she ministers and
who lovingly and sacrificially reaches out
to share or help bear the
pains and problems of others
even as he or she joyously proclaims
God's love and heaven's blessings
as revealed through Jesus Christ.

We accept Luther's assertion that
"We are all beggars—
that is the truth,"
and we may agree with Daniel Niles'
metaphorical definition of evangelism
as "One beggar telling
another beggar where to find bread."
It is, of course, more than that.
Evangelism is
the proclamation and revelation of the good
and joy-giving news of
God's loving and reconciling grace
to humanity all about us.
This was the intention

of Jesus when He sent out the seventy
disciples on a sort of trial run
in respect to their ministry as
His followers
(Luke 10:1–9).
"I am sending you out like
lambs among wolves,"
He said, referring to their confrontation
with an evil-infested,
conflict-ridden world.
They were sent out two-by-two.
They were expected to place
themselves at God's disposal
and be guided by His Spirit.
They were simply to go out
and share God's love with people.
They were to speak
to people in a friendly way,
showing them their genuine concern for them.
They were to accept
the hospitality of those whom they
visited—to stay in one home,
sharing their food and drink.
They were to listen
to them, to accept and
seek to understand them, and
to share of themselves with them—
even to the point of disclosing their own
needs and concerns with these people and to
accept what was given to them.
When the confidence of these people was won,
their host would begin to reveal to them
his problems and troubles,

the needs of his household.
After a relationship had been established
    and the needs of the household became known,
    Jesus enjoined His representatives
    to "heal the sick."
    This may have referred to
    whatever sickness or dis-ease that
    afflicted that household:
    a quarrel to be resolved,
    divisions to be reconciled,
    a deep-seated fear to be confronted and eliminated,
    some darkness or depression or
    anxiety or loneliness or purposelessness that
    ought to be dealt with.
Then the evangelists are commanded to
    proclaim the great and good news that
    the Kingdom of God is close to you—God
    is here and is ready
    to envelop you in His everlasting grace.
God has come into the world through
    Jesus Christ and is ready
    to forgive and redeem,
    set free and empower
    everyone who turns to Him and who
    accepts Him and His purposes
    for their lives.

Like the seventy disciples of our Lord's day,
    we too are thrust out, like
    lambs in the midst of wolves, into
    our kind of world.
We are to seek out those people
    to whom we can relate,

to listen to them, accept
them, share with them.
We are to "heal the sick" or
use every means within our power
and the equipment and power God grants to us
to meet these people and to
minister to these people.
We may be able to
heal their loneliness,
raise them out of despair,
restore their dignity,
help them find jobs, or
provide for some of their material needs
that may alleviate their suffering.
We are, of course, expected
to do everything possible in
relating them to that one who is
the answer to their deepest needs.
He is the one who can
accept, forgive, heal, and restore
them to His life and purposes.
Evangelism is indeed our task.

There are risks involved.
We will not always see
the result of our witness to some
of those within
our arena of responsibility.
Our great God did not
promise visible results,
only an open door
of opportunity and the charge
to be faithful and obedient to

our calling as His ministers
and servants.
Yet—
We have been redeemed and empowered to
    communicate the healing and
    saving love of God to a distraught world.
Where there is hatred, we must sow love.
Where there are wounds, we are to grant healing.
Where there is despair, we can proclaim hope.
Where there is darkness, we must shed light.
Where there is death, we will proclaim life
    in Jesus Christ.
And we are equipped
    by the grace of God to do
    these very things—and thereby to
    bring a bit of heaven *now*
    into the lives of people in our path.

Our Commitment to the Kingdom of God

If anyone would come after Me,
he must deny himself and
take up his cross
and follow Me.—Mark 8:34

The faith and fervor of the original
    Christians, the intense passion and power
    of those first followers of
    the resurrected Christ,
    the devotion and drive manifest in
    the waking hours of the church,
    are hard to come by in our generation.
The Christianity we have often
    been a part of and contributed to
    has been a kind of streamlined
    facsimile of the real thing,
    a guilty conscience
    in exchange for a soft cushion of
    comfort and consolation, or a kind of defensive,
    crawling-into-our-holes-to-lick-our-wounds
    Christianity.
This was not true of original
    Christianity nor the Christ of Christianity.
While Jesus at times may have been
    tempted to settle for something
    less than a genuine commitment to
    the plan and purposes of His heavenly Father,
    this was a temptation to which

He never yielded.
While there was often a crowd following
    Him in His earthly sojourn and ministry—
    mostly out of curiosity or
    seeking signs and miracles—
    He persisted in sifting those crowds
    and discouraged any lighthearted adherence to
    Him or His principles and
    often faced the multitudes only
    to drench with cold water
    the too-easily-kindled flame.
He even issued plain statements about
    the painful consequences that would befall
    those who continued to follow Him.

We have inherited and probably supported
    from time to time
    numerous cults and cubbyholes that
    specialize in some narrow aspect or
    incident of Christ's life and ministry:
    healing,
    comfort,
    peace,
    eternal security,
    forgiveness of sin,
    deliverance
    from some addiction—
    all of which may be essential, but still
    may not embrace the whole Gospel or really
    express the full meaning of
    the Gospel and the cost
    involved for those who truly
    follow Jesus Christ.

Our Lord consistently preached for commitment.
He never expected that His followers
      would get by with anything
      less than total commitment.
It was, no doubt, this
      kind of preaching that limited His following to
      a mere handful of publicans and fishermen.
When the crowds pressed in upon Him
      following His feeding-of-the-five-thousand
      miracle, He tried to tell them that
      He was the bread of life and only
      those who identified with
      Him and His purposes would ever know
      the real meaning of life.
They left Him in droves (see John 6:30–58).
Even many of our generation who
      should know better consign
      His "eat my flesh"
      and "drink my blood" analogy
      to weekly Communion services
      and assume that such fulfills their
      obligations to be
      identified with and committed to
      Jesus Christ.
At one time or another during
      His ministry,
      Jesus told His followers
      they had better count the cost if
      they were going to be His disciples.
      Jesus stressed that His purposes
      for the lives of His followers
      must take precedence over their
      country, parents, mates, children—

even their own lives.
"Any of you who does not
give up everything he [or she]
has cannot be My disciple"
(Luke 14:25–33).

Abraham was called
    to get out of his country and
    his father's house that
    he might be of use to God.
Moses had to turn his back
    on those who raised him in order that
    he might be free to serve his God.
Jeremiah was expected
    to deny himself the greatest joys of
    this life, such as wife and children,
    in order to follow God's plan for his life.
Our God may never call us
    to do what He expected of these
    ancient servants,
    but whatever
    His word to us and His will for us,
    it may be better that we
    make no decision at all
    to follow Jesus if
    that decision is to be a halfhearted one.

Many of us have faced up to
    Christ's total claims upon our
    lives from the time we were taught
    about the Christian faith but
    may have read into those claims what
    we wanted them to say—

or just ignored them altogether.
As a consequence
of our apathetic and rather ephemeral
relationship to our Savior and Lord,
we may have become a part
of a tea-and-crumpets,
country-club Christianity that
bears no resemblance whatsoever to
the pattern for discipleship that
Jesus inaugurated.

Whatever may be
our spiritual temperature at the moment,
we need to recognize who
we are and where we stand in
our relationship to God.
It may mean that we
who call ourselves followers of Christ
must throw out our adulterated concepts
of discipleship and become authentic
in our relationship to God.
This will necessitate our return
to His word and will
for our lives.

There is nothing easygoing
about the kind of life and
committal that Jesus prescribes.
It is costly and demanding.
It promises
not softness but suffering,
not comfort but challenge,
not safety but sacrifice.

There *is* peace.
There is also persecution.
There *is* security, joy, enrichment.
There is also blood, sweat, and tears.
Our response to God's great gift of love and
    to Christ's call to servanthood
    and ministry must be
    commitment.
We can't be effective
    even in our secular goals and projects
    without commitment.
And yet all of these things are
    really only our avocation.
Our vocation is to serve
    God, follow our Lord, to
    be Christs-incarnate
    in our kind of world along with
    all our Christian brothers and sisters,
    ministers and servants of
    the almighty God.
    And that vocation
    deserves and demands
    total commitment.

Of course there are risks involved;
    at least they appear to be risks
    in this three-dimensional world in which we live.
    But the risk of being
    lost to God or left out of His
    purposes for our lives is
    far greater for those who
    never move out of the cubbyhole of
    their initial spiritual experience and

onto the battleground of conflict and
change that comes through bringing heaven
now into the kingdom of this world.
Of course there will be
failures in our determination to
live committed lives, but there is
always forgiveness and renewal when we fall
and the grace of God that enables us
to get up and try again.
And as committed Christians, maturing
Christians, there is life and truth,
purpose and objective,
reconciliation and renewal.

Our Witness to *Heaven/Now*

Therefore, since we have a great high priest
who has gone through the heavens,
Jesus the Son of God, let us hold firmly
to the faith we profess. . . .
Let us then approach the throne of grace
with confidence, so that we may receive
mercy and find grace to help us
in our time of need.—Heb. 4:14, 16

There was once a lawyer who
      wanted to know how he could be
      guaranteed of heaven.
      "What is written in the Law?"
      asked Jesus of the lawyer.
      " 'Love the Lord your God
      with all your heart
      and with all your soul
      and with all your strength
      and with all your mind,'
      and 'Love your neighbor as yourself,' "
      responded the lawyer.
      "You have answered correctly," said Jesus.
      "Do this and you will live."
This lawyer was not about to
      challenge the ancient and
      revered commandment,
      but he was as cagy
      as the best of us and probably more
      honest than many of us in posing

the question, "And who is my neighbor?"
We do not know if our Lord's
answer was a surprise to the lawyer,
but His recital of the parable
of the Good Samaritan (Luke 10:30–36)
may well be a revealing and
judgmental condemnation upon some of us.
The lawyer may have assumed that
no one could challenge his love for God.
After all,
he said the right words;
he went through the required motions.
He probably carried on
a respectable sort of life.
But the second half of the commandment—
love of neighbor—
stopped him cold.
That was where the authenticity of
his faith could be challenged.
He had only one recourse:
"Who is my neighbor?"

It may be that
the story of the Good Samaritan tends to make
much of our professed and assumed piety
appear to be something
less than authentic.
Of course salvation is a gift.
It cannot be earned or merited.
It must be accepted as God's
gift as it is proclaimed and
demonstrated by Jesus Christ.
We can't earn a love that is already granted.

We can only embrace it
by faith or neglect to accept it.
It is when we truly open our lives to
God's love that we become
channels and communicators
of divine love toward our neighbor.

However, in our emphasis upon
the subjective,
the personal relationship to Christ,
we still may have neglected
the second great precept
and consequence of
a vital and valid Christianity,
the other side of the gospel coin:
our relationship to our neighbor.
This may be the reason some of us are
reluctant to face the
import of the Great Commandment.
It challenges the profession, the
expression, of our faith and reveals
the authenticity and validity of our beliefs.

We recognize the importance of
the Great Commandment, the need
to proclaim the Gospel.
We have invested money and
talents in the ongoing
task of bringing the Gospel of
Jesus Christ to the whole world.
If we ever cease preaching
Jesus Christ crucified and risen
from the dead,

and His power to save
and the peoples' need for
His salvation,
we had better demit and begin
selling something useful—
like encyclopedias or life insurance.

On the other hand,
    if all we do is recite Scripture,
    send Bibles,
    pray,
    and pass offering plates,
    it is not surprising that the
    deprived, displaced,
    oppressed, and poverty-stricken
    masses of the world—
    and even the unchurched
    people of our own neighborhoods—
    fail to respond
    to this limited kind of witness.

There is no question whatsoever about
    the why and what for
    of our salvation.
    It comes from God; it comes as a gift.
It is not enough, however,
    to say the right words
    like "I love You, Jesus," or
    "I accept You, Christ."
    There must be the placing of
    ourselves at God's disposal,
    the presentation of our bodies
    as living sacrifices

(see Rom. 12:1).
This is not mere words; it is an action.
And the only way that we can really
act in this manner toward
our invisible God is to
commit ourselves to the
valid needs of our visible neighbor.

Who is our neighbor?
Our Lord gave the answer—loudly and clearly.
Every human being is our neighbor—
and this without regard to color,
background,
or social status.
Christ's overall command is to
preach the Gospel
to every creature.
The personal requirement, and
the ministry and assignment
for every Christian, is to
love his or her fellow beings.
If we think this is
overemphasized or exaggerated,
we need only to heed God's
Word in the words of John, who
declared that "Anyone who does
not love
remains in death"
(1 John 3:14).
And this may be true regardless
of how much Scripture that person
quotes or how much he or she
prays or gives to

favorite charities.
Who is our neighbor?
Lonely senior citizens in rest homes,
    deserted wives with children underfoot and Mother
    Hubbard cupboards,
    the couple breaking up next door,
    the starving and homeless all over this planet,
    drug addicts,
    immigrants, and people
    of every color and race.
    These are our neighbors.
    God's command is that we love
    them, reach out to
    them, not only with words, but
    with Christ-impelled actions.
When Jesus concluded the Good Samaritan parable,
    He referred to the three
    men who confronted the victim,
    "Which of these three
    do you think was a neighbor to the
    man who fell into the hands of robbers?"
    "The one who had mercy on him,"
    responded the lawyer.
    Jesus said to him, "Go and do
    likewise."

"Go and do likewise!"
Maybe this is a rather simplistic
    approach to the meaning of love,
    but it is usually where it begins.
    This is our assignment and our witness.
We can carry out this assignment through
    our denominational structures that can

reach out to the hungry and oppressed masses
of people throughout our world;
through our social and political
agencies that organize to relate to
the needs of people in our crowded cities;
through our congregations that can zero in on
specific needs in their respective communities.
Above all, we should be doing this through the personal
touch where we can,
through our love,
reach out in love
to others around us and,
inspired and empowered
by God's love,
introduce people to
the redeeming love
of God as revealed
through the crucifixion
and resurrection of
Jesus Christ.

When we believe that Jesus Christ
is our Savior and Lord,
we know that God has
taken care of our salvation.
We know that heaven is
our eventual destiny.
In the meantime, God has
an assignment for us to
carry out in this fractured world.
This includes the command and
the task of loving our neighbor and
dramatizing that love at the point of

his or her immediate need.
Above all is the command of Jesus Christ
and the glorious privilege of directing that
person or persons to the love
and grace of God through Jesus Christ, who
died on the cross to reveal God's
forgiveness of their sins and who
arose from the dead to reveal and present
them with the gift of eternal life.
This is the way in which we can
bring heaven into our world
now, and to involve
ourselves and others in God's eternal
Kingdom forever.

God comes to His human creatures
on this planet in diverse ways.
He comes to a hungry family
by way of a loving friend or
neighbor bearing a bag of groceries,
to a homeless child
through a person or agency offering
shelter to a victim of loneliness and despair,
by way of a stranger who takes the time to offer
compassion and friendliness.
We cannot count the ways in which
God reveals His love
to His creatures and brings
heaven's light into the darkness of human
misery;
and He does such even through those who are totally
unaware of His presence and activity
through these good deeds.

"Christ [and heaven's blessings] comes
    to and through broken flesh,
    the bypassed heart, . . .
    the ears that hear,
    the eyes that read lips,
    the healing voice,
    the arms embracing,
    the face of rival or friend," wrote one author.
It is, however, through His own
    redeemed sons and daughters
    that God reveals His saving love and
    His gift of everlasting
    life to all who will come to Him.
This task is not limited
    to ordained pastors or trained teachers,
    but is the privilege and the task
    of every child of God.
We are to declare that
    the Kingdom of God has come,
    that by way of Jesus Christ,
    His cross and His resurrection,
    God has come to
    His fallen creatures to restore them
    to His life and purposes, and
    to forgive, redeem, and reinstate them
    in His will and objectives
    for their lives.
We are to proclaim the Good News
    of God and heaven,
    to invite God's creatures
    about us to become a part of God's
    family and recipients of His Kingdom's gift
    and to dedicate their lives

to serving Him by becoming His
servants to others around them.
"Let us, then, go to Him outside the camp,
bearing the disgrace He bore.
For here we do not have an enduring city,
but we are looking for the city that is to come.
Through Jesus, therefore, let us continually
offer to God a sacrifice of praise—
the fruit of lips that confess His name.
And do not forget to do good and to
share with others, for with such
sacrifices God is pleased"
(Heb. 13:13–16).

We have, by faith in the forgiving love
of God as revealed through Jesus Christ,
already inherited heaven
now.
While the full revelation
of heaven will be made following
our life and service on this planet,
shadows, glimpses, flashes, even
incomprehensible and inexplicable visions
of heaven have and will continue
to come to us even
now.

May God grant to each of us the grace
to respond to His everlasting
love and to live and serve as genuine
followers of Christ in our world today.

Epilogue

This is not the time for despair;
    it is the time for celebration!
Jesus has come;
    He is present with
    us amidst the trials
    and tribulations of this tempestuous world.
He will soon come again and gather His
    faithful followers
    into the fully revealed and eternally
    reigning Kingdom of God.
The "marriage supper of the Lamb"
    is about to take place, and
    the suffering, celebrating, faithful
    children of God
    of all nations and generations are invited.
Christ will, once and for all time,
    reveal Himself as the
    living, overcoming, victorious
    Lord of heaven and earth.
Evil will be eradicated;
    all stumbling blocks will be removed;
    those who oppose God and His people
    will be overcome;
    the spiritual forces of evil will be
    bound and destroyed.
Sorrow will turn to joy, night into day.
Tears will give way to laughter.
It is on this great Day that
    the suffering martyrs,

the struggling saints,
the priests and prophets,
servants and disciples of all the ages
shall be united
together to sing their praises to their eternal
Savior and King.

Words cannot describe it—
this fantastic event
about to take place.
But God's faithful children—
clothed in His righteousness—
can believe it and hope for it
and ready themselves for it,
because it will happen,
and all the pain and suffering
that encompassed them in this
world will be forgotten in the glorious
revelation of Christ as King
in the world to come.
Jesus is about
to return and
take His church to Himself.
He is coming soon!
Let us begin the celebration even now!

(Adapted from *Prophets/Now*)